MEXICO

Recipes, Flavors & Traditions

P.J. Tierney

KITCHEN INK

KITCHEN INK's passionate Kids in the Kitchen team of recipe creators, testers, editors, food stylists, photographers, and designers work tirelessly to create products that introduce kids to cooking. Having fun, making memories in the kitchen, and creating a delicious meal is what we are all about.

Our easy-to-follow, creative, and delicious recipes—kid-tested and parent-approved—include both healthy meals and special treats. Adult supervision and safety first are always important in the kitchen. We hope you enjoy our books as much as we have loved creating them.

Library of Congress Cataloging-in-Publication data is available.
ISBN 978-1-943016-24-2

First Edition
28 29 27 26 25   10 9 8 7 6 5 4 3 2 1

Printed in China

Kitchen Ink Publishing
114 John Street, #277
New York, NY 10038

Kitchen Ink books may be purchased for educational, business, or sales promotional use. For information, please email the Special Markets Department at sales@kitcheninkpublishing.com.

See what Kitchen Ink is up to, share recipes and tips, and shop our store—www.kitcheninkpublishing.com.

  kitcheninkpublishing

For Nik

With fond memories of
our Mexican adventures
and a lifelong friendship.

Introduction by P.J. Tierney

I always return from Mexico with fond memories. The vibrant colors, traditional music, delicious food, warm and welcoming people, and nightlife always guarantee a great time. Relaxing on the beautiful beaches (wearing sunscreen) while reading a book is a dream. Sprinkle in a bit of history by visiting the well preserved Chichén Itzá, an ancient Mayan city in the Yucatan peninsula built around 250 AD to 900 AD. At over 4 square miles (10 square km), it's one of the largest Mayan cities ever built. At its peak, it was home to over 35,000 people.

Mexican food is available worldwide as fast food and at more traditional Mexican restaurants where you can enjoy dining while listening to the music of a mariachi band. Cooking traditional Mexican recipes at home is not only fun, but also a delicious way to share with the whole family. Many of the recipes in this book serve a lot of people. Add a piñata and have a party!

The Tortilla recipe on page 22 is made from four simple ingredients and is the base of many Mexican recipes, including Chicken Fajitas on page 49, Enchiladas de Pollo on page 46, and Baked Chicken Chimichangas on page 60.

For many of these recipes, you can choose chicken, beef, or vegetable filling. Make Pechugas de Pollo (Chicken Breasts in Stock) on page 62 and add rice for a delicious meal. Or use this chicken for your Chimichangas, Enchiladas, or many other recipes in this book. Along with traditional Mexican recipes, I've included a new recipe that's sure to become a family tradition. Bake the delicious Chocolate Piñata Cake on page 82 and surprise and delight everyone when this delicious cake is cut and candy spills out. This recipe is a bit more challenging to make, and you will need patience to cut, fill, and frost the cake. When you complete this recipe, you have earned a blue-ribbon sticker for your Culinary Passport.

Frida Kahlo captured the flavor of Mexico in her artwork. Of her more than 200 paintings, 55 are self-portraits, and you could say she created the first "selfie." In her lifetime, she painted a few commissioned portraits for money but sold only a handful of paintings. Several years ago, Frida's 1949 self-portrait, "Diego y yo," sold at auction for $34.9 million. Turn to page 87 to learn more about this true Mexican treasure.

Day of the Dead is a Mexican tradition to celebrate the lives of those who have died. Once a year, families and friends welcome the spirits back with favorite foods, photos, elaborate altars, music, and lots of love. Food is an important part of this holiday and read more about it on page 89.

Pan de Muerto (Bread of the Dead), on page 32, is the most traditional food you could eat on Day of the Dead. This very sweet bread is covered with sugar and decorated with bone-like shapes on the front. Most stores in Mexico sell large quantities of Pan de Muerto during the holiday to adorn home altars and to share amongst friends. Choose how to decorate your own Day of the Dead Cookies on page 72. I opted for fun skull faces using pastel colors and heart candy. Make these cookies and you have earned a Day of the Dead sticker for your Culinary Passport.

It's hard to choose a favorite recipe from this wonderful collection. There are recipes for every occasion: breakfast, small plates, salsas & sides, entrées, and desserts. The Fiesta Taco Salad on page 44 always satisfies, and I like the combination of lettuce and crunch. May I suggest Sweet Potato Nachos with Black Beans and Cheese on page 35? Or the Elotes (Mexican Street Corn), on page 30, which can be served on its own or is delicious as a side. Whip up a batch of Guacamole on page 28, and serve it with chips. For a party, add a trio of salsas: Mango, Serrano, and Avocado, on page 24; Roasted Tomatillo Cilantro, on page 26; and Golden Pico de Gallo on page 27. Have fun making Queso Fundido with Chorizo on page 38. You may not have ever eaten Cactus Salad before, so give it a try on page 18 and you have earned a sticker for your Culinary Passport.

Play with your food? Yes, please! Cookie cutters in the shapes of letters can be used to prepare the Buñuelos recipe on page 80. Spell out a word, a name, or cut a heart shape into the Tortillas prior to frying them. Then arrange the letters on a platter to spell out your message. I recommend I 🖤 MOM or DAD.

Thanks for joining me on this culinary adventure. Enjoy!

P.J. Tierney

A Note from the Kids in the Kitchen Team

Each recipe notes the number of servings and the time needed to prepare the dish. Please note, the recommended chilling time for a dish may not be included in its active preparation time.

This cookbook includes easy recipes and those requiring a little more patience and skill. As you become more comfortable preparing recipes, it is important to be challenged and improve your kitchen skills.

An adult should be with you to assist, especially when using a knife and the stovetop, and when putting your delicious dishes into and bringing them out of the hot oven. It is up to the adult to decide when you can be more independent in the kitchen.

Step-by-step directions tell you what you need to prepare the dish. Read each recipe completely before you begin and make sure you have all the tools and ingredients you need. These recipes are written for kids all around the globe and both US measurements and metrics are included.

Sometimes a recipe may call for an ingredient you do not have. A substitution will be offered for an international ingredient that may be challenging to find. Please note if an ingredient is marked "optional," you can leave it out of the recipe if you choose.

If you are vegetarian, you will find recipes without meat or with suggestions to prepare meatless versions of the dish.

Everyone is excited to taste the food they have created BUT hit the brakes. Food is piping hot when removed from the oven. Always be patient and let the food cool before sampling. Your tongue will thank you.

Always clean up the kitchen when you are done and remember that more hands make light work. Have a cleanup party and everyone is rewarded with dessert.

Contents

Breakfast

Small Plates, Salsas & Sides

Entrées

Desserts

Breakfast

Avocado Toast

 15 minutes   4 servings

Ingredients

4 slices of bread, your choice

2 ripe avocados

1 lime, juiced

½ teaspoon (2.5 milliliters) cumin

¼ teaspoon (1.2 milliliters) chili powder

¼ teaspoon (1.2 milliliters) salt

¼ teaspoon (1.2 milliliters) pepper

1 small tomato, diced

½ red onion, chopped

2 tablespoons (30 milliliters) fresh cilantro, chopped

4 radishes, sliced

½ cup (120 milliliters) queso fresco, crumbled

2 jalapeños, pickled

2 tablespoons (30 milliliters) hot sauce, optional

Directions

1. Toast the bread slices until golden in color and crisp.

2. In a medium bowl, mash the avocados with a fork.

3. Add the lime juice, cumin, chili powder, salt, and pepper and mix well to combine.

4. Spread the avocado mixture equally onto each slice of toasted bread.

5. Top the avocado with tomatoes and red onion.

6. Layer the toast with cilantro, radishes, queso fresco, jalapeños, and hot sauce, if using.

7. Serve immediately.

Breakfast Burritos

 40 minutes

 4 servings

Ingredients

4 large eggs

¼ teaspoon (1.2 milliliters) smoked paprika

¼ teaspoon (1.2 milliliters) salt

½ pound (0.23 kg) spicy sausage (chorizo, Italian sausage, or any type you like), removed from casings

1⅓ cups (320 milliliters) Monterey Jack cheese, shredded

4 10-inch (25.4-centimeter) flour tortillas

Vegetable oil

TIP

Add salsa. Choose one from pages 24 to 26.

Directions

1. In a medium bowl, whisk the eggs with the smoked paprika and salt. Set aside.

2. Heat a large nonstick pan over medium-high heat. Add the sausage and cook, stirring frequently until browned, 4 to 5 minutes. Remove the sausage from the pan with a slotted spoon, reserving drippings in the pan.

3. In a small bowl, scramble the eggs and add to the pan, reducing the heat to low. Cook the eggs until cooked through and light and fluffy.

4. Assemble the burrito: Spoon ¼ cup of salsa of your choice on top of the tortilla. This recipe is for 4 burritos, and you will divide the sausage and eggs into 4 portions. On top of the salsa add a quarter of the sausage, a quarter of the eggs, and ⅓ cup (80 milliliters) of cheese.

5. Fold the sides of the tortilla over the filling and roll, tucking in the edges as you go. Repeat with all 4 tortillas.

6. Lightly coat the pan with oil and set over medium heat. When the pan is hot, add the burritos, seam-side down. Cook, covered, until the burrito is golden brown, about 3 minutes. Flip the burritos over and continue cooking. Serve warm.

Chilaquiles

 30 minutes　　 4 servings

Ingredients

Red Sauce

3 tablespoons (45 milliliters) canola oil

½ sweet onion, diced

2 garlic cloves, minced

2 cups (280 milliliters) crushed tomatoes

6 chipotles in adobo sauce

2/3 cup (160 milliliters) unsalted chicken stock

Fried Eggs

2 tablespoons (30 milliliters) extra-virgin olive oil

4 eggs

Salt and pepper to taste

Chilaquiles

8 ounces (224 grams) tortilla chips

Garnishes

½ cup (120 milliliters) queso fresco, crumbled

2 radishes, thinly sliced

½ bunch cilantro leaves, roughly chopped

Directions

Red Sauce

1. In a large skillet, over medium-high heat add oil.

2. Add onion and garlic and sauté for 2 to 3 minutes. Reduce heat to medium and continue to cook for another 2 minutes. Season with salt and pepper.

3. Pour mixture into a blender and add crushed tomatoes, chipotle peppers with adobo sauce, and stock. Blend until smooth.

4. Pour the sauce back into the skillet and simmer over medium-low heat for 10 minutes.

Fried Eggs

1. Place a large skillet over medium-high heat and add oil. Crack eggs into the skillet and fry eggs for 3 to 4 minutes or until the edges of the eggs are crispy and the yolks are still runny. Remove from heat and set aside.

Chilaquiles

1. Raise the heat of the red sauce to medium-high and bring to a boil for about 3 minutes. Add tortilla chips, a handful at a time. Gently folding in to cover with sauce.

2. Continue to add chips to the sauce until all are evenly coated. Season with salt and pepper. Remove from heat and top with fried eggs.

3. Garnish with queso fresco, radishes, and cilantro. Serve immediately.

Sweet Corn Pancakes with Cinnamon Honey Butter

 30 minutes   4 servings

Ingredients

Pancakes

1 cup (240 milliliters) flour

1 cup (240 milliliters) cornmeal

2 tablespoons (30 milliliters) sugar

2 teaspoons (10 milliliters) baking powder

½ teaspoon (2.5 milliliters) salt

1 cup (240 milliliters) milk

½ cup (120 milliliters) canned corn, rinsed and drained

2 large eggs

2 tablespoons (30 milliliters) melted butter

1 teaspoon (5 milliliters) vanilla extract

Cinnamon Honey Butter

4 tablespoons (60 milliliters) butter, softened

2 tablespoons (30 milliliters) honey

½ teaspoon (2.5 milliliters) ground cinnamon

Directions

1. In a large mixing bowl, whisk together flour, cornmeal, sugar, baking powder, and salt.
2. In another large bowl combine milk, corn, eggs, butter, and vanilla.
3. Pour the wet ingredients into the dry ingredients and stir until just combined. Let the batter rest for 5 minutes.
4. In a small bowl, mix butter, honey, and ground cinnamon.
5. Preheat a skillet over medium heat and grease with cooking spray.
6. Spoon ¼ cup (60 milliliters) of batter onto the skillet for each pancake. Cook until bubbles form, then flip and cook until golden brown.
7. Repeat with the remaining batter.
8. Serve warm, topping with Cinnamon Honey Butter.

Mexican Hot Chocolate Oatmeal

 20 minutes

 2 servings

Ingredients

2 cups (480 milliliters) rolled oats

4 cups (960 milliliters) milk

2 tablespoons (30 milliliters) unsweetened cocoa powder

2 tablespoons (30 milliliters) brown sugar

¼ teaspoon (1.2 milliliters) ground cinnamon

¼ teaspoon (1.2 milliliters) chili powder

¼ teaspoon (1.2 milliliters) salt

Directions

1. In a medium saucepan over medium heat, combine the rolled oats, milk, cocoa powder, brown sugar, ground cinnamon, chili powder, and salt. Bring the mixture to a gentle boil, stirring occasionally to prevent sticking.

2. Once the mixture reaches a boil, reduce the heat to low and simmer for about 5 to 7 minutes, or until the oats have cooked and the mixture has thickened.

3. Stir occasionally to ensure even cooking. Remove the saucepan from the heat and let it sit for a minute to cool slightly. Serve warm.

Poblano Breakfast Potatoes

 50 minutes

 6 servings

Ingredients

2 potatoes, scrubbed and cut into ¼-inch (0.6-centimeter) wide chunks

1 poblano pepper, seeds removed and diced

½ onion, diced

4 garlic cloves

2 tablespoons (30 milliliters) olive oil

1 teaspoon (5 milliliters) salt

Black pepper, freshly ground

½ teaspoon (2.5 milliliters) hot chili powder, optional

Directions

1. Preheat the oven to 425°F (220°C). Line a baking sheet with parchment paper.
2. In a large mixing bowl, combine the potatoes, pepper, onion, and garlic, oil, salt, and pepper. If using, add the chili powder.
3. Spread the mixture in an even layer on the prepared baking sheet.
4. Bake for 30 to 40 minutes, carefully stirring to move the potatoes around to cook on all sides.
5. Remove from the oven and serve.

Small Plates, Salsas & Sides

Cactus Salad with Avocado Dressing

 30 minutes   4 servings

Ingredients

¼ onion, chopped

2 garlic cloves, smashed

1 teaspoon (5 milliliters) dried oregano

¼ teaspoon (1.2 milliliters) salt

4 cups (960 milliliters) water

6 cups (1,440 milliliters) prickly pear cactus paddles, cleaned and chopped

1 avocado, halved, pitted, and peeled

½ cup (120 milliliters) cilantro, divided

3 tablespoons (45 milliliters) extra-virgin olive oil

½ serrano chili, stemmed and seeded

1 ½ tablespoons (22.5 milliliters) distilled white vinegar

2 tablespoons (30 milliliters) water

¼ teaspoon (1.2 milliliters) ground black pepper or to taste

½ cup (120 milliliters) seeded plum tomatoes, chopped

¼ cup (60 milliliters) queso fresco or feta cheese, crumbled

⅓ cup (80 milliliters) scallions, chopped

Directions

1. In a saucepan over high heat, combine the onion, garlic, oregano, salt, and water and bring to a boil. Once at a rolling boil add the cactus and boil for 7 minutes, or until tender and no longer bright green. Strain the cactus and place it on a plate to cool down.

2. To make the dressing, in the container of a blender add avocado, ¼ cup (60 milliliters) of cilantro, oil, chili, vinegar, and water, and blend until very smooth and thick. Season to taste with salt and pepper.

3. Transfer the cactus to a salad bowl and add the tomatoes, cheese, scallions, and ¼ cup (60 milliliters) chopped cilantro and toss to combine.

4. Pour dressing over salad to coat, and toss gently. You can always add more. Divide the salad onto 4 plates. Include dressing on the side so people can decide how much to use.

TIP
If you can't locate fresh cactus, use canned.

Arroz a la Mexicana (Mexican Rice)

 50 minutes

 6 servings

Ingredients

2 cups (480 milliliters) long-grain rice

4 cups hot water

1 large tomato, peeled and seeded

½ medium onion, quartered

2 cloves garlic

⅓ cup (80 milliliters) light oil

¼ teaspoon salt

4 cups (960 milliliters) of chicken broth or 2 cups broth and 2 cups water

½ cup (120 milliliters) peas

Avocado slices

Directions

1. In a medium bowl, add rice and cover with hot water and let it stand to swell for about 15 minutes, then drain off water. Rinse rice several times with cold water until the water runs clear. Drain rice well, put in a bowl, and set aside.

2. In a blender add tomato, onion, garlic, and puree.

3. In a large skillet, over medium-high heat add oil. Add rice to coat grains and fry rice, stirring until rice is golden all over.

4. Add the puree and continue to fry and stir until the rice is dry. Add salt and pour the broth over the mixture. Stir once and lower heat to a simmer.

5. Cover and continue to cook for approximately 20 minutes without stirring, until broth is absorbed.

6. Let rest for 10 minutes, then stir in hot cooked peas, and serve garnished with avocado slices.

Tortillas

 30 minutes   12 servings

Ingredients

1 ¼ cups (300 milliliters) whole-grain flour

¼ cup (60 milliliters) butter, cut into small pieces

⅝ cup (150 milliliters) warm water

1 tablespoon (15 milliliters) olive oil

Directions

1. Sift the flour into a large bowl. Add the butter and stir in the water. Mix until well combined and a dough is formed. Rub olive oil over dough ball, place in a bowl, and cover with a towel for 20 minutes.

2. Flour a flat surface and divide the dough into 12 balls.

3. Roll out each ball into 5 ½-inch (13.75 centimeters) circles.

4. In a heavy skillet, heat a small amount of oil. Place a tortilla in the pan, cooking it for 2 minutes, and flipping it over to cook another 2 minutes.

5. Add the topping of your choice, tear a tortilla to dip in a salsa, or use it for enchiladas, tacos, or fajitas.

Mango, Serrano, and Avocado Salsa

 15 minutes

 3 cups (720 milliliters)

Ingredients

1 mango, peeled, pitted, and diced

2 avocados, halved, pitted, peeled, and diced

1 serrano chili, charred, stemmed, seeded, and diced

1 tablespoon (15 milliliters) cilantro, chopped

2 teaspoons (10 milliliters) fresh lime juice

¼ teaspoon (1.2 milliliters) salt

¼ teaspoon (1.2 milliliters) freshly-ground black pepper

Directions

1. In a large bowl, add the mangos, avocados, chili, cilantro, lime juice, salt, and pepper. Mix well.

2. Serve immediately.

TIP
Have an adult char the chili by placing the chili on a metal skewer and gently turn over the flame of the stovetop to brown on all sides.

Roasted Tomatillo Cilantro Salsa

 25 minutes

 2 ½ cups (600 milliliters)

Ingredients

1 ½ pounds (0.68 kilograms) tomatillos, husked, rinsed, and halved

2 small white onions, quartered

1 serrano chili, halved, stemmed, and seeded

2 tablespoons (30 milliliters) olive oil

¼ teaspoon (1.2 milliliters) salt

¼ teaspoon (1.2 milliliters) pepper

1 garlic bulb, wrapped tightly in aluminum foil

1 cup (240 milliliters) chicken broth

½ avocado, halved, pitted, peeled, and diced

3 tablespoons (45 milliliters) fresh cilantro, chopped

Directions

1. Preheat oven to 350°F (180°C).
2. In a medium bowl, add the tomatillos, onions, and serrano chili and olive oil. Gently fold until all is covered in olive oil.
3. Pour the contents of the bowl onto a baking sheet.
4. Add the foil-wrapped garlic on the baking sheet.
5. Roast for 45 minutes, or until all vegetables are soft and beginning to brown. The garlic is done when soft. Remove the baking sheet from the oven to cool.
6. Transfer the tomatillos, onions, and serrano chili to the container of a blender.
7. Unwrap the garlic and squeeze the garlic cloves into the blender.
8. Add the broth to the blender, and puree all to a chunky texture.
9. Pour into a medium bowl, and fold the avocado and cilantro into the salsa.

Golden Pico de Gallo

 15 minutes   3 cups (720 milliliters)

Ingredients

1 ½ pounds (0.68 kilograms) yellow tomatoes, seeded and chopped

¾ cup (175 milliliters) onion, chopped

½ cup (120 milliliters) fresh cilantro, chopped

3 tablespoons (45 milliliters) fresh lime juice

2 serrano chilies, stemmed, seeded, and minced

¼ teaspoon (1.2 milliliters) salt

¼ teaspoon (1.2 milliliters) freshly-ground black pepper

Directions

1. In a medium bowl, add the tomatoes, onion, cilantro, lime juice, and serrano chilies. Mix to combine. Season with salt and pepper.
2. Cover and chill for at least 30 minutes.

Guacamole

 20 minutes 2 cups

Ingredients

2 ripe avocados

½ teaspoon (2.5 milliliters) salt

1 garlic clove, finely minced

1 teaspoon (5 milliliters) fresh lime juice or to taste

1 medium-sized tomato, chopped

¼ cup (60 milliliters) finely chopped red onion

1 medium-sized jalapeño, minced

2 tablespoons (30 milliliters) fresh cilantro, coarsely chopped

Directions

1. Halve and pit the avocados, and scoop pulp into a medium bowl.

2. Add salt and garlic; add lime juice to taste.

3. Fold in tomato, onion, jalapeño, and cilantro. Let stand a few minutes before serving to allow flavors to blend. Taste and adjust seasonings as necessary.

Elotes (Mexican Street Corn)

 20 minutes   4 servings

Ingredients

4 fresh ears of corn, husked

¼ cup (60 milliliters) of mayonnaise

¼ cup (60 milliliters) sour cream

½ cup (120 milliliters) cotija cheese, crumbled

1 teaspoon (5 milliliters) chili powder

¼ cup (60 milliliters) fresh cilantro, chopped

1 lime, cut into wedges

Salt and pepper to taste

Directions

1. Preheat a grill pan over medium heat. Grill the corn, turning occasionally until the corn is lightly charred on all sides, about 8 to 10 minutes.

2. In a small bowl, mix together mayonnaise and sour cream to create the crema.

3. Once the corn is grilled, brush each ear with the crema.

4. Sprinkle the crumbled cheese over the corn, followed by a dusting of chili powder.

5. Garnish with chopped cilantro and serve with lime wedges on the side. Season with salt and pepper.

Pan de Muerto – Bread of the Dead

 2 hours 35 minutes   1 loaf

Ingredients

2 ¼ teaspoons (11.2 milliliters) dry yeast

½ cup (120 milliliters) lukewarm water

5 cups (1,200 milliliters) flour

1 teaspoon (5 milliliters) salt

½ cup (120 milliliters) sugar

1 cup (240 milliliters) butter, melted and cooled

6 eggs, lightly beaten

2 tablespoons (30 milliliters) of anise water, see recipe below

2 tablespoons (30 milliliters) orange blossom water

1 tablespoon (15 milliliters) grated orange rind

Egg Wash

1 egg

1 tablespoon (15 milliliters) water

1 tablespoon (15 milliliters) milk

Glaze

1 ½ cups (360 milliliters) powdered sugar

1 teaspoon (5 milliliters) vanilla exctract

1 teaspoon (5 milliliters) milk

Pink sugar crystals, for dusting, optional

> **TIP**
> Have fun! Traditional designs are bones -roll dough into two small logs. Using fingers, shape the dough to form two bones. Cross the bones across the top of the bread loaf.

Directions

1. In a glass measuring cup, dissolve yeast in water.

2. In a medium bowl, add 1 cup (240 milliliters) of the flour and pour in the yeast and water. Stir to combine and cover with a cloth and let rise in a warm place. The dough should double in size.

3. In a medium bowl, combine butter, eggs, anise water, orange blossom water, and orange rind.

4. Reserve ½ cup (120 milliliters) of flour and set aside.

5. Add the remaining flour, salt, and sugar to the dough and mix to combine. Add in the egg mixture and mix well.

6. Sprinkle a flat surface with the remaining flour and remove the dough. Place it on the prepared surface.

7. Flour clean hands and lightly knead the dough. Place dough in a greased bowl and set in a warm place for 1 ½ hours to rise.

8. Preheat the oven to 350°F (180°C).

9. Shape dough into a round loaf. Reserve a bit of the dough to decorate the loaf.

10. Dust the work surface with flour and roll all leftover dough into small balls and place these balls on top of the bread loaf.

11. In a small bowl, combine the egg and water and brush the bones, balls, and top and sides of bread loaf with this egg wash.

12. Bake for 30 minutes and allow to cool.

13. In a small bowl, mix powdered sugar, vanilla, and milk to form a glaze.

14. Once cooled, pour the glaze over the top of the bread loaf and sprinkle with pink sugar crystals.

Anise Water

1. In a small pot over medium heat, add 1 tablespoon anise seeds to ¼ cup (60 milliliters) of water. Simmer for 3 to 4 minutes and then strain off the seeds.

Sweet Potato Nachos with Black Beans and Cheese

 40 minutes

 4 servings

Ingredients

2 large sweet potatoes, sliced

115-ounce (425 grams) can black beans, rinsed

1 cup (240 milliliters) cheddar cheese, shredded

¼ cup (60 milliliters) tomatoes, diced

¼ cup (60 milliliters) red onion, diced

1 cup (240 milliliters) fresh cilantro, chopped

1 jalapeño, thinly sliced, optional

¼ cup (60 milliliters) sour cream, optional

1 tablespoon (15 milliliters) olive oil

1 teaspoon (5 milliliters) ground cumin

¼ teaspoon (1.2 milliliters) chili powder

¼ teaspoon (1.2 milliliters) salt

¼ teaspoon (1.2 milliliters) pepper

Directions

1. Preheat the oven to 425° F (220°C).

2. In a large bow,l toss sweet potato with olive oil, cumin, chili powder, salt, and pepper.

3. Line a baking sheet with parchment paper and spread out the potatoes. Bake for 20 to 25 minutes until lightly browned and crispy. Remove from the oven to slightly cool.

4. In a small bowl, combine tomatoes, onion, cilantro, and jalapeño if using.

5. Top each potato round with black beans and cheddar cheese and return the baking sheet to the oven until the cheese melts.

6. Transfer the bean and cheese-topped potatoes to a platter. Pour the tomato mixture evenly over all the potatoes and top with sour cream, if desired. Serve immediately.

Queso Fundido with Chorizo

 25 minutes   4 servings

Ingredients

8 ounces (224 grams) chorizo, casings removed

1 small onion, finely chopped

2 garlic cloves, minced

1 tomato, diced

½ teaspoon (2.5 milliliters) ground cumin

½ teaspoon (2.5 milliliters) smoked paprika

8 ounces (224 grams) Monterey Jack cheese, shredded

2 tablespoons (30 milliliters) fresh cilantro, chopped

Directions

1. In a skillet over medium heat, cook the chorizo until browned. Set aside.
2. In the same skillet, sauté onions until translucent, add garlic, and cook for 1 minute.
3. Stir in tomato, cumin, and paprika and cook for 2 to 3 minutes.
4. Return cooked chorizo to the skillet and cook for another 2 to 3 minutes.
5. Reduce heat to low and sprinkle cheese over the mixture. Stir until melted and bubbly.
6. Garnish with cilantro and serve immediately.

Grilled Corn and Poblano Potato Salad

 50 minutes

 8 servings

Ingredients

2 pounds (0.9 kilograms) red-skinned potatoes

3 ears fresh corn, husks removed

2 poblano chilies, charred, peeled, stemmed, seeded, and chopped

½ cup (120 milliliters) sour cream

¼ cup (60 milliliters) mayonnaise

¼ cup (60 milliliters) fresh cilantro, chopped

Salt

Pepper, freshly ground

Directions

1. To char the chilies, have an adult place the chilies into a broiler and after 3 minutes turn over to ensure both sides are blackened.

2. In a large pot, fill with water, salt, and potatoes. Cover and bring to a boil and cook for 30 minutes, or until potatoes are tender when pierced. Drain the potatoes and let cool. Once cooled, cut the potatoes in half.

3. Using a grill or grill pan, over medium-high heat carefully place the ears of corn and grill, turning the ears, until browned on all sides, for 10 minutes. With adult supervision and a sharp knife remove the corn kernels from the corncobs and into a large bowl.

4. Add the potatoes, chilies, scallions, sour cream, mayonnaise, and cilantro, and combine.

5. Season to taste with salt and pepper.

Entrées

Fiesta Taco Salad

 30 minutes

 4 servings

Ingredients

Salad

1 pound (0.45 kilograms) ground beef

1 tablespoon (15 milliliters) olive oil

1 small onion, diced

2 garlic cloves, minced

1 tablespoon (15 milliliters) taco seasoning

¼ teaspoon (1.2 milliliters) salt

¼ teaspoon (1.2 milliliters) pepper

4 cups (960 milliliters) shredded lettuce

1 cup (240 milliliters) cherry tomatoes, halved

1 cup (240 milliliters) canned black beans, drained

1 cup (240 milliliters) frozen corn kernels, thawed

½ cup (120 milliliters) black olives, sliced

½ cup (120 milliliters) shredded cheddar cheese

Dressing

¼ cup (60 milliliters) sour cream

2 tablespoons (30 milliliters) mayonnaise

1 teaspoon (5 milliliters) lime juice

1 teaspoon (5 milliliters) taco seasoning

Directions

1. In a large skillet, heat olive oil over medium heat. Sauté onion and garlic until fragrant and translucent.

2. Add ground beef and cook until browned, breaking up into crumbles.

3. Sprinkle the taco seasoning over the meat, season with salt and pepper, and stir to coat evenly. Cook for 2 to 3 minutes, remove from heat, and set aside.

4. In a large salad bowl, combine lettuce, tomatoes, beans, corn, olives, and shredded cheese.

For the dressing, in a small bowl whisk sour cream, mayonnaise, lime juice, and 1 teaspoon (5 milliliters) taco seasoning.

Enchiladas de Pollo (Chicken Enchiladas)

 55 minutes 5 servings

Ingredients

4 scallions, sliced, divided

4 ounces (110 grams) diced chilies

2 cups (480 milliliters) diced or shredded cooked chicken

1 cup (240 milliliters) frozen corn, thawed

½ cup (120 milliliters) salsa, plus more for serving

⅓ cup (80 milliliters) sour cream

10 corn tortillas, 6-inches (15-centimeters)

1 ½ cups (360 milliliters) shredded Mexican cheese

Directions

1. Preheat the oven to 400°F (200°C). Spray a 9 x 13-inch (23 x 33-centimeter) baking dish with cooking spray. Spread ½ cup (120 milliliters) enchilada sauce in the bottom of the dish.

2. In a medium bowl, combine 2 scallions, chiles, chicken, corn, salsa, and sour cream.

3. Warm 5 tortillas in the microwave for 20 to 30 seconds until soft. Spoon ¼ cup (60 milliliters) filling onto the center of a tortilla. Roll up and set, seam-side down, in the prepared baking dish. Repeat with the remaining warmed tortillas. Warm the remaining 5 tortillas and continue filling them and arrange them into the casserole dish. Spread the remaining sauce over the enchiladas.

4. Transfer to the oven and bake for 15 minutes. Top with cheese and continue baking until the enchiladas are steaming hot all the way through, the sauce is bubbling, and the cheese is melted, about 10 minutes longer. Let cool for 10 minutes before serving. Garnish with the remaining scallions prior to serving.

Enchilada Sauce

 10 minutes   2 cups (480 milliliters)

Ingredients

3 tablespoons (45 milliliters) olive oil

3 tablespoons (45 milliliters) flour

1 tablespoon (15 milliliters) ground chili powder

1 teaspoon (5 milliliters) ground cumin

½ teaspoon (1.5 milliliters) garlic powder

¼ teaspoon (1.2 milliliters) dried oregano

¼ teaspoon (1.2 milliliters) salt, to taste

Pinch of cinnamon, optional

2 tablespoons (30 milliliters) tomato paste

2 cups (480 milliliters) vegetable broth

1 teaspoon (5 milliliters) apple cider vinegar or distilled white vinegar

Freshly-ground black pepper, to taste

Directions

1. In a medium bowl, add flour, chili powder, cumin, garlic powder, oregano, salt, and cinnamon (if using) and set aside.

2. In a medium-sized pot over medium heat, warm the oil until it's hot enough that a light sprinkle of the flour/spice mixture sizzles on contact.

3. Once it's ready, pour in the flour and spice mixture. While whisking constantly, cook until fragrant and slightly deepened in color, about 1 minute. Whisk the tomato paste into the mixture, then slowly pour in the broth while whisking constantly to remove any lumps.

4. Raise heat to medium-high and bring the mixture to a simmer, then reduce heat as necessary to maintain a gentle simmer. Cook, whisking often, for about 5 to 7 minutes, until the sauce has thickened (the sauce will thicken some more as it cools).

5. Remove from heat, then whisk in the vinegar and season to taste with freshly-ground black pepper. Add more salt, if necessary.

Chicken Fajitas

 55 minutes   4 servings

Ingredients

For the Chicken

1¼ to 1 ½ pounds (0.56 to 0.68 kilograms) skinless, boneless chicken breasts

Salt

2 tablespoons (30 milliliters) oil of your choice - canola, safflower, peanut, or extra-virgin olive oil

1 large onion, sliced lengthwise, root to tip, into ¼-inch (0.6-centimeter) strips

3 bell peppers of various colors, sliced into ¼-inch (0.6-centimeter) strips

For the Marinade

2 tablespoons (30 milliliters) lime juice

3 tablespoons (45 milliliters) extra-virgin olive oil

1 garlic clove, minced

½ teaspoon (2.5 milliliters) salt

½ teaspoon (2.5 milliliters) ground cumin

½ teaspoon (2.5 milliliters) chili powder

½ jalapeño, seeded and minced

¼ cup (60 milliliters) chopped cilantro

For Serving

8 to 12 flour tortillas

Salsa

1 avocado, sliced

Sour cream

Iceberg lettuce, thinly sliced and lightly salted and sprinkled with cider vinegar

Directions

1. Cut chicken breasts in half horizontally then cut into ½-inch (1.25-centimeter) thick strips.

2. In a medium bowl, add the lime juice, olive oil, garlic, salt, cumin, chili powder, jalapeño, and cilantro and mix well. This is the marinade.

3. In a glass bowl, combine the marinade and the chicken and mix well. Cover and let marinate at room temperature for 30 minutes.

4. Remove the chicken from the marinade and wipe off most of the marinade and sprinkle the chicken pieces with salt.

5. In a large cast iron frying pan, heat 1 tablespoon of oil on high heat for 1 minute. When the oil begins to smoke, lay the chicken pieces in the pan. Let the chicken cook undisturbed for 2 to 3 minutes, until you have a good sear. Once seared well on one side, turn the pieces over and cook for another 2 to 3 minutes until well seared on the second side.

6. Once seared on the second side, remove the chicken to a cutting board and cover with aluminum foil to rest for 5 minutes.

7. Add another tablespoon of oil to the frying pan and heat on high. As soon as the oil is hot, add the onions and peppers to the pan. Cook for 2 minutes and stir peppers and cook for another 2 minutes.

8. Serve the chicken with the peppers and onions, some warm tortillas, and sides of shredded cheese, salsa, guacamole, and/or thinly sliced iceberg lettuce dressed with vinegar and salt.

Hearty Mexican Beef Stew

 2 hours　　　 4 servings

Ingredients

1 pound beef stew meat, cubed

2 tablespoons vegetable oil

1 onion, chopped

2 garlic cloves, minced

2 carrots, peeled and sliced

2 potatoes, peeled and diced

1 bell pepper, diced

1 cup corn kernels

1 14-ounce (392 grams) can diced tomatoes

3 cups beef broth

1 teaspoon cumin

1 teaspoon chili powder

½ teaspoon dried oregano

¼ teaspoon salt

¼ teaspoon pepper

2 tablespoons fresh cilantro, chopped

Directions

1. In a large pot, heat the vegetable oil over medium heat.

2. Add the beef and brown on all sides. Remove from the pot and set aside.

3. In the same pot, add the onion and garlic and sauté until translucent, approximately 3 minutes.

4. Return the browned beef to the pot and add cumin, chili powder, oregano, and salt and pepper. Stir to coat. Pour in the broth and diced tomatoes and simmer for approximately 1 hour or until the beef is tender.

5. Add the carrots, potatoes, bell pepper, and corn. Simmer for 30 to 40 minutes or until the vegetables are cooked to desired tenderness.

6. Garnish with cilantro and serve.

Fish Tacos

 30 hours   24 tacos

Ingredients

24 small white corn tortillas

1½ pound tilapia

½ teaspoon ground cumin

½ teaspoon cayenne pepper

1 teaspoon salt

¼ teaspoon black pepper

1 tablespoon olive oil

1 tablespoon unsalted butter

Toppings

½ small purple cabbage

2 medium avocados, sliced

2 roma tomatoes, diced, optional

½ diced red onion

½ bunch cilantro, longer stems removed

4 ounces 1 cup cotija cheese, grated

1 lime cut into 8 wedges to serve

Taco Sauce Ingredients

½ cup sour cream

⅓ cup mayonnaise

2 tablespoon lime juice, from 1 medium lime

1 teaspoon garlic powder

1 teaspoon sriracha sauce, or to taste

Directions

1. Line a large baking sheet with parchment or silicone liner. In a small dish, combine cumin, cayenne pepper, salt, and black pepper and evenly sprinkle seasoning mix over both sides of tilapia.

2. Lightly drizzle fish with olive oil and dot each piece with butter. Bake at 375°F (190°C) for 20 to 25 minutes. To brown edges, broil for 3 to 5 minutes, if desired.

3. Combine sour cream, mayo, lime juice, garlic powder, and siracha sauce in a medium bowl and whisk until well blended.

4. To serve the tacos, toast the corn tortillas quickly on a large dry skillet or griddle over medium/high heat.

5. To assemble: start with pieces of fish then add remaining ingredients, finishing with a generous sprinkling of cotija cheese and top with taco sauce.

6. Serve with a fresh lime wedge to squeeze over tacos.

Chilies Rellenos (Stuffed Peppers)

 1 hour

 4 servings

Ingredients

4 fresh poblano chile peppers

½ pound (0.23 kilograms) lean ground beef

1 onion, chopped

1 clove garlic, chopped

¼ teaspoon (1.2 milliliters) salt

¼ teaspoon (1.2 milliliters) pepper

3 eggs, separated

1 cup (240 milliliters) shredded mozzarella cheese

2 roma (plum) tomatoes, chopped

½ cup (120 milliliters) all-purpose flour

1 cup (240 milliliters) corn oil

DEFINITION
Sweating is a way of softening vegetables over moderate heat, in oil or fat until vegetables become soft.

Directions

1. Have an adult place whole peppers over an open flame, gas burner, or under the broiler. Roast, turning frequently until evenly black and blistered. Remove from heat, place in a plastic bag, and let them sweat for a while. This will allow the skins to peel off easily.

2. While the peppers are sweating, in a large skillet over medium-high heat, cook the beef, stirring to crumble, until evenly browned. When beef is fully cooked, add the onion, garlic, and tomato, and cook for a few more minutes. Season with salt and pepper.

3. Remove the peppers from the bag, and peel off the burnt skin. You may wish to wear protective gloves. Run peppers under cool running water to rinse away any burnt pieces. Make a small vertical slit in the side of each pepper, and remove the seeds and veins. Stuff each pepper halfway with the ground beef mixture, then fill the rest of the way with shredded cheese. Close the slits, and secure them with toothpicks.

4. Whip egg whites in a large glass or metal bowl until thick and fluffy. Add the egg yolks, and whip for a minute to blend.

5. Meanwhile, heat ¼-inch (0.6-centimeters) of oil in a large heavy skillet over medium-high heat. Coat the stuffed peppers with a light dusting of flour, then dip them in the egg so they are fully covered. Carefully place in the hot oil, and fry on both sides until golden. Drain on paper towels, then serve on a large platter.

Baked Chicken Chimichangas

 40 minutes 4 servings

Ingredients

2 cups (480 milliliters) cooked chicken, shredded

1 tablespoon (15 milliliters) chili powder

½ teaspoon (2.5 milliliters) cumin

¼ teaspoon (1.2 milliliters) paprika

½ teaspoon (2.5 milliliters) salt

½ cup (120 milliliters) salsa

2 cups (480 milliliters) Colby-Jack cheese, shredded

2 ounces (56.7 grams) cream cheese, softened

2 tablespoons (30 milliliters) green onions, chopped

1 15-ounce (425 grams) can refried beans

4 10-inch (25-centimeter) tortillas

1 tablespoon (15 milliliters) olive oil

Directions

1. Preheat the oven to 400°F (200°C).

2. In a medium-sized mixing bowl, combine chicken, chili powder, cumin, paprika, salt, salsa, Colby-Jack cheese, cream cheese, and green onions.

3. For each tortilla, spoon 2 tablespoons (30 milliliters) onto tortilla 2 inches (5 centimeters) from the edge. Put about ½ cup (120 milliliters) of meat mixture into the center. Fold in sides of tortilla, roll up the bottom, and place seam-side down on a baking sheet. Brush tops with olive oil. Bake for 20 minutes or until golden brown and heated through.

4. Serve warm.

Pechugas de Pollo (Chicken Breasts in Stock)

 45 minutes

 4 servings

Ingredients

1 carrot, chopped

1 celery stalk, chopped

1 garlic clove

Small bunch of fresh parsley

2 chicken breasts, bone in

4 cups (960 milliliters) water

½ small white onion

1 teaspoon (5 milliliters) salt

¼ teaspoon (1.2 milliliters) freshly-ground pepper

TIP
Use this chicken to make tacos, enchiladas, burritos, or add it to a side of rice.

Directions

1. In a 4-quart stockpot, add carrot, celery, garlic, parsley, chicken, water, onion, salt, and pepper.
2. Reduce the heat to low and simmer for 35 to 40 minutes, or until the chicken is tender and cooked through. Skim off any foam that rises to the top during cooking.
3. Drain the chicken into a strainer.
4. After the chicken has cooled, discard the skin, and shred the chicken.

Pork Posole

 2 hours

 4 servings

Ingredients

1 pound (0.45 kilograms) pork shoulder, cubed

1 tablespoon (15 milliliters) vegetable oil

1 onion, diced

3 garlic cloves, minced

2 teaspoons (10 milliliters) ground cumin

1 teaspoon (5 milliliters) dried oregano

1 teaspoon (5 milliliters) chili powder

15 ounces (425 grams) hominy, rinsed

4 cups (946 milliliters) water

¼ teaspoon (1.2 milliliters) salt

¼ teaspoon (1.2 milliliters) pepper

TIP
Hominy is whole or ground kernels of corn from which hull and germ have been removed. A substitute could be chickpeas, sweet corn, barley, brown rice, wild rice, or polenta.

Directions

1. In a large pot, over medium heat warm vegetable oil.
2. Add the onion and garlic and sauté until the onion is soft and translucent.
3. Add the pork and cook until browned on all sides.
4. Stir In the cumin, oregano, and chili powder and cook for 1 minute.
5. Pour in the hominy and 4 cups (960 milliliters) of water and bring mixture to a boil.
6. Reduce the heat, cover, and simmer for 1 to 1 ½ hours, or until the pork is tender.

Desserts

Mexican Chocolate Sugar Crisps

 40 minutes 54 servings

Ingredients

¾ cup (175 milliliters) shortening

1¼ cups (300 milliliters) sugar, divided

1 large egg, room temperature

¼ cup (60 milliliters) light corn syrup

2 ounces (57 grams) unsweetened chocolate, melted and cooled

1¾ cups (415 milliliters) all-purpose flour

1½ teaspoons (7.5 milliliters) ground cinnamon

1 teaspoon (5 milliliters) baking soda

¼ teaspoon (1.2 milliliters) salt

1 cup (240 milliliters) semisweet chocolate chips

Directions

1. Preheat oven to 350°F (180°C).

2. In a large bowl, cream shortening and 1 cup (240 milliliters) sugar until fluffy, 5 to 7 minutes. Beat in egg, corn syrup, and melted chocolate. In another bowl, whisk flour, cinnamon, baking soda, and salt; gradually beat into creamed mixture. Stir in chocolate chips.

3. Shape dough into 1-inch (2.5-centimeter) balls; roll in remaining sugar. Place dough balls 2 inches (5 centimeters) apart on ungreased baking sheets. Bake until the tops are puffed and cracked, 8 to 10 minutes. Cool on pans for 2 minutes. Remove to wire racks to cool.

Mexican Wedding Cookies

 45 minutes 36 servings

Ingredients

1 cup (240 milliliters) butter, softened

½ cup (120 milliliters) powdered sugar

1 teaspoon (5 milliliters) vanilla extract

2 ¼ cups (1,020 milliliters) sifted flour

¼ teaspoon (1.2 milliliters) salt

¾ cups (175 milliliters) walnuts or pecans, chopped

Powdered sugar, for dusting

Directions

1. Preheat oven to 400°F (200°C).

2. In a medium bowl, cream together butter and powdered sugar until light and fluffy; stir in vanilla.

3. In a bowl, whisk together flour and salt; add gradually to butter mixture; stir in chopped nuts.

4. Chill dough if it seems too soft.

5. Form dough into 1 ¼-inch (3.1-centimeter) balls and place onto parchment-lined or ungreased baking sheets.

6. Bake for 10 to 12 minutes or just until the cookies start to turn light golden brown. Remove from oven and allow to cool slightly. While cookies are still warm (but NOT hot), remove them from baking sheets and roll, a few at a time, in powdered sugar until evenly coated. Cool cookies completely on wire racks.

7. Roll cookies in powered sugar, optional.

Day of the Dead Cookies

 2 hours 10 minutes

 12 cookies

Ingredients

1 ¼ cups (300 milliliters) butter, softened

1 ¾ cups (400 milliliters and 1 tablespoon) powdered sugar

2 ounces (56.7 grams) almond paste

1 large egg, room temperature

¼ cup (60 milliliters) 2% milk

1 teaspoon (5 milliliters) vanilla extract

4 cups (960 milliliters) all-purpose flour

½ teaspoon (2.5 milliliters) salt

2 12-ounce (340 grams) packages white candy-coating melts

Optional decorations: jumbo sprinkles, peppermint candies, and brown food coloring (for our cookies we used pink sprinkles)

TIP

You choose how to decorate your cookies. Try black and dark colors for a scary look, or pastel colors (like our cookies) with pink sprinkles and candies.

Directions

1. In a large bowl, cream butter and powdered sugar until light and fluffy; add almond paste. Beat in the egg, milk, and vanilla. Combine flour and salt; gradually add the creamed mixture and mix well. Cover and refrigerate for 1 hour.
2. Preheat oven to 375°F (190°C).
3. On a lightly floured surface, roll out dough to ¼- inch (0.6-centimeter) thickness. Cut out with a 5-inch (12.5-centimeter) skull-shaped cookie cutter. Place 1 inch (2.5 centimeters) apart on ungreased baking sheets.
4. Bake in the oven for 7 to 9 minutes or until firm. Let stand for 2 minutes before moving to wire racks to cool completely.
5. In a large shallow microwave-safe dish, add the white candy melts and microwave at 50% power or defrost setting for 1 minute. Stir thoroughly and continue to microwave at the same setting, stirring until the candy is almost completely melted. If there are small pieces that haven't melted, let candy sit for about 1 minute.
6. Dip the top side of each cookie into coating, allowing excess to drip off, and place on waxed paper.
7. Decorate as desired. Tint remaining white candy-coating brown; pipe on mouth and let stand until set. We used pink sprinkles and hearts for eyes.

Tres Leches Cake

 4 hours 35 minutes   12 servings

Ingredients

For the Cake

Unsalted butter for greasing pan

12 ounces (340 grams) sweetened condensed milk

12 ounces (340 grams) evaporated milk

1 cup (240 milliliters) heavy cream

1 cup (240 milliliters) all-purpose flour

1 cup (240 milliliters) sugar

1 teaspoon (5 milliliters) baking powder

¼ teaspoon (1.2 milliliters) salt

3 large eggs

¼ cup (60 milliliters) whole milk

1 teaspoon (5 milliliters) vanilla extract

Whipped cream, for topping

For the Whipped Cream

1 cup (240 milliliters) heavy cream

2 tablespoons (30 milliliters) sugar

¼ teaspoon (1.2 milliliters) vanilla extract

Directions

1. Preheat the oven to 350°F (180°C). Grease a 12-cup muffin pan with butter.
2. Grease a 9 x 13-inch (23 x 33-centimeter) glass baking dish with the butter. Add the condensed milk, evaporated milk, and heavy cream, and mix until well combined. Set aside.
3. In a large bowl, whisk together flour, granulated sugar, baking powder, and salt.
4. In a medium bowl, whisk the eggs, milk, and vanilla until well combined.
5. Pour the egg mixture into the flour mixture and whisk gently to moisten the batter.
6. Divide the batter evenly into the 12 muffin cups. Bake 18 to 20 minutes or until the cakes are golden in color and a wooden skewer inserted into the middle comes out clean.
7. Remove the cupcakes from the oven and poke each several times with the skewer.
8. Carefully remove each cupcake from the pan and place in the baking dish with the milk and cream. Spoon the milk and cream mixture over each cake. Let the soaked cupcakes cool completely, soaking up the milk for about 1 hour.
9. Transfer the cakes to an airtight container and cover tightly.
10. Pour the remaining milk and cream mixture in a separate container and cover.
11. Store both containers in the refrigerator.
12. Continue to pour the milk mixture over the cakes until soaked. Can refrigerate up to 2 days prior to serving.

Whipped Cream

1. Whip the heavy cream, sugar, and vanilla until thick and spreadable.
2. Spread over the cake surface. Decorate cake with whole or chopped maraschino cherries. Cut into squares and serve.

Champurrado (Mexican Hot Chocolate)

 10 minutes   4 servings

Ingredients

¼ cup (60 milliliters) baking cocoa

2 tablespoons (30 milliliters) brown sugar

1 cup (240 milliliters) boiling water

¼ teaspoon (1.2 milliliters) ground cinnamon

Dash ground cloves or nutmeg

3 cups (720 milliliters) whole milk

1 teaspoon (5 milliliters) vanilla extract

Whipped cream

Whole cinnamon sticks

Directions

1. In a small saucepan, mix cocoa and sugar; stir in water. Bring to a boil. Reduce heat; cook 2 minutes, stirring constantly.

2. Add cinnamon and cloves; stir in milk. Simmer 5 minutes (do not boil). Whisk in vanilla. Pour hot chocolate into mugs; top with whipped cream. Use cinnamon sticks for stirrers.

Buñuelos

 25 minutes

 6 servings

Ingredients

½ cup sugar

1 teaspoon ground cinnamon

Vegetable oil, for frying

6 8-inch tortillas

Directions

1. On a plate, mix the sugar and cinnamon together.

2. In a medium saucepan, pour in enough oil to reach halfway up the sides.

3. Heat the oil to 350°F (180°C).

4. Working in batches, with an adult, fry the tortillas in the hot oil for 2 minutes on each side, until golden brown.

5. Transfer them to paper towels to drain.

6. While still warm, toss the tortillas with the cinnamon and sugar.

7. Serve warm.

TIP

Have fun! Use cookie cutters to spell out your name, the word "LOVE", or "Mexico."

Chocolate Piñata Cake

 2 hours 5 minutes

 12 to 14 slices

Ingredients

Chocolate Cake

1½ cups (195 grams) all purpose flour

¾ cup (85 grams) natural unsweetened cocoa

1 teaspoon (5 milliliters) baking soda

½ teaspoon 2.5 milliliters) salt

½ cup (120 grams) unsalted butter, room temperature

½ cup (120 milliliters) vegetable oil

1½ cups (310 grams) sugar

1½ teaspoons (310 grams) vanilla extract

4 large eggs

1¼ cups (300 milliliters) milk

Chocolate Buttercream Frosting

1¼ cups (280 grams) unsalted butter, room temperature

1¼ cups (237 grams) shortening

¾ teaspoon (3.70 milliliters) salt

9 cups (1035 grams) powdered sugar

2 teaspoons (10 milliliters) vanilla extract

4 to 5 tablespoons (60 to 75 milliliters) water or milk

1 cup (240 milliliters) natural unsweetened cocoa powder

> **TIP**
> Fill the cake with your favorite small candy.

Ingredients, continued

Chocolate Ganache

1 cup (240 millimeters) semisweet chocolate chips

½ cup (120 millimeters) heavy whipping cream

Additional

Mini Reese's pieces

Mini chocolate chip cookies

M&Ms

Directions

1. Preheat oven to 350°F (176°C) and prepare three 8-inch cake pans with nonstick baking spray and parchment paper in the bottom.
2. Combine the flour, cocoa, baking soda, and salt in a medium-sized bowl and set aside.
3. Add the butter, oil, sugar, and vanilla extract to large mixing bowl and beat together until light in color and fluffy, about 3 to 4 minutes. Do not skimp on the creaming time.
4. Add the eggs one at a time, mixing until mostly combined after each. Scrape down the sides of the bowl as needed to be sure all ingredients are well incorporated.
5. Add half of the dry ingredients to the batter and mix until mostly combined.
6. Slowly add the milk and mix until well combined. The batter will look curdled, but that's ok.
7. Add the remaining dry ingredients and mix until well combined and smooth. Scrape down the sides of the bowl as needed to be sure all ingredients are well incorporated. Do not overmix the batter.
8. Divide the batter evenly between the prepared cake pans and bake for 19 to 21 minutes, or until a toothpick comes out with a few moist crumbs.
9. Remove cakes from the oven and allow to cool for 2 to 3 minutes, then remove to a cooling rack to finish cooling.
10. To make the frosting, beat together the butter, shortening, and salt until smooth.

11. Slowly add 4 cups (460 grams) of powdered sugar and mix until smooth.

12. Add the vanilla and half of the water or milk and mix until smooth.

13. Add the other 5 cups (575 grams) of powdered sugar and mix until smooth.

14. Add the cocoa and mix until smooth.

15. Add the remaining water or milk until the frosting is stiff enough to hold its shape, but spreadable enough to easily frost your cake.

16. To build the cake, you'll need something to cut through the cake layers— 3-inch biscuit cutter, round cookie cutter, or a sharp knife would be fine too. Cut a hole all the way through one of the cake layers. You can the hole to be in the center of the cake.

17. For the other two cake layers, cut a hole only about halfway through the cake layer and then use a spoon to carefully remove the cake within the marking.

18. Place one of the cake layers with only a partial hole onto a cake plate or cardboard cake circle and spread about ½ cup of frosting around the top of the cake, on the outside of the hole.

19. Place the next cake layer on top – the one with the full hole removed – then add another layer of frosting.

20. Spread a thin layer of frosting around the side of the hole of the cake, then fill the cake with your choice of candies and treats. You should fill the hole so everything sticks above the sides of the hole just a bit. The next layer of cake has a partial hole, so that extra filling/ treats will fill in that space.

21. Add the final layer of cake on top, then frost the outside of the cake.

22. To make the ganache topping, add the chocolate chips to a medium-sized bowl.

23. Add the heavy whipping cream to a microwave-safe measuring cup and microwave until it just begins to boil.

24. Pour the hot cream mixture over the chocolate chips and let it sit for 2 to 3 minutes, then whisk until smooth.

25. Drizzle the chocolate ganache around the edges of the cake, then fill in the center/top of the cake.

26. Use the remaining frosting to pipe swirls around the edge of the cake, then top the cake with additional candies.

Frida Kahlo

"I paint self-portraits because
I am so often alone, because
I am the person I know best."
—Frida Kahlo

Frida Kahlo was an artist who has had a significant impact on Mexican art. She remains one of the most iconic and celebrated artists in Mexican history, known for her love of Mexico and its culture, and for courage in the face of adversity.

Her work is celebrated for its bold use of vibrant color, symbolism, and its representation of the female experience. Kahlo's paintings often use a folk style with vibrant red, white, and green, which are the colors of her beloved Mexican flag. For self-portraits, Kahlo wears peasant clothing with flowers in her hair.

Magdalena Carmen Frida Kahlo y Calderón was born on July 6, 1907 in Coyoacaón, a village on the outskirts of Mexico City. Frida Kahlo's father, a professional photographer, was born in Germany and became a naturalized Mexican citizen because of his love for his adopted country. Her Mexican mother was of Spanish and Native American descent. Frida's parents were passionate about art, literature, and music, which influenced her own love of art. She also found inspiration in the nature and artifacts of Mexico.

At the age of six, Kahlo suffered from polio. The disease made her right leg thinner than her left one, and its decreased circulation caused her chronic pain. She was bedridden, and isolated for nine months. Frida wore long skirts in the traditional Mexican style to cover her leg, and these long skirts became part of her trademark. At age 18, she nearly died in a bus accident. She suffered multiple fractures and began to focus heavily on painting while recovering in a body cast.

Frida's life experiences, and her emotional and physical pain, are common themes in her approximately 200 paintings and sketches. Fifty-five of these are self-portraits.

At the Frida Kahlo Museum in Mexico City, Frida's personal belongings are on display. It is the most popular museum in the Coyoacaón neighborhood, and among the most visited in all of Mexico City. The museum is housed in the building Kahlo was born and grew up in. It has cobalt blue walls and so is nicknamed the Blue House. She lived in this home with her husband, the celebrated Mexican artist Diego Rivera. This home is where she lived, painted, and died in 1954 at the age of 47.

Frida Kahlo's legacy has brought international recognition to Mexican art and has increased people's interest in visiting Coyoacaón and learning more about Mexican culture.

Is Day of the Dead a scary occasion?

No, Day of the Dead (Dia de Muertos) is a very important and significant celebration of LIFE. On the first day of November each year, it is a time to welcome back the spirits of loved ones who have died. Those who have lost loved ones celebrate "with them" once more. The Day of the Dead celebration dates back more than 2,500 years to pre-Columbian times. It's an opportunity to remember people and share memories with the younger generations who may not have known the person or their importance in a family's history.

All over Mexico streets shut down, and houses are filled with loved ones, flowers, delicious food, and traditional music.

Mexico, Flavors, Recipes, and Traditions highlights the following traditional recipes to celebrate Day of the Dead:

Pan de Muerto (Bread of the Dead) on page 32 – decorate this bread as you wish. Creating bone shapes from the dough and crossing them on top of the bread is most popular.
Pork Posole – on page 64
Day of the Dead Cookies on page 72 – you get to choose how to decorate these skull cookies
Tres Leches Cake – on page 75
Champurrado (Mexican Hot Chocolate) on page 78

Altares (Altars)

On the last day of October, altars are displayed in public places, but the most religious families put altars in their homes to welcome back the spirits. Ferns are placed on the floor to create a soft path to the altar, with candles lighting the way. Photos of loved ones, favorite fruit, bread, candy, cookies, toys, and presents are placed on the altar to offer to the spirit. It's also traditional to include food that that the loved one most enjoyed. Some families also decide to prepare a dinner of everything their loved ones used to really like to eat themselves.

Marigolds, the most traditional flower of the holiday, are placed on altars and graves. Altars are quite beautiful, and there are contests for the most elaborate ones.

November 1st, All Saints Day, is dedicated to children. November 2nd is for adults. Graveyards are filled with families celebrating the departed. Picnics take place over graves, music is played, and graves are adorned with flowers.

After Day of the Dead is over, the *ofrenda* food is typically consumed by the living family members and friends who have gathered to remember and honor their departed loved ones. It is believed that the spirits of the deceased have absorbed the spiritual essence of the food, and the physical portion is then enjoyed by the living as a way to continue the connection with their loved ones. Since the dead only require a small portion, the living must finish the dish in order not to waste the food.

La Catrina

A symbol representative of Day of the Dead is La Catrina, a skeleton illustration of death, often wearing Mexican clothing with Mexican cultural elements. People participate in festivals to spread the spirit of the holiday all over Mexico.

Día de los Muertos is, above all, a celebration of family. Sadness, anxiety, and loss are replaced with music, colors, dancing, and food to remember and honor the dead.

The Culinary Passport Series

With 35 delicious, easy-to-make recipes for breakfast, small plates, sides & snacks, entrées, and desserts.

Full color photos and cooking tips.

Let's get cooking!

Pasta with Tomato Sauce Allo Scarpariello

25 minutes | 4 servings

Ingredients

11 ounces\312 grams Penne or Spaghetti

9 ounces\255 grams cherry tomatoes, cut in half

15 ounces\425 grams tomato puree

¼ cup\60 milliliters Parmigiano

¼ cup\60 milliliters Parmigiano Reggiano cheese, grated

Basil, a handful, washed and torn into pieces

⅓ cup\80 milliliters Extra virgin olive oil

Garlic, 1 clove, peeled

Fine salt, to taste

Directions

1. In a large pot, boil a pot of salted water.

2. In a large frying pan heat the olive oil and sauté garlic until it softens and add some basil.

3. Add the tomatoes when the tomatoes have softened, pour in the tomato puree.

4. Simmer for approx 15 minutes, remove the garlic and add salt and pepper to taste.

5. Add pasta to the pot of boiling water and cook al dente, drain it and add to the saucepan. Cook for 2-3 more minutes until the pasta is cooked.

6. Lower the heat and add the cheese and combine with sauce and pasta. Cheese should melt in.

7. Serve immediately with fresh basil and extra cheese.

Empanadas

30 minutes | 4 servings

Ingredients

For the dough

3 cups\720 milliliters all-purpose flour, plus more for surface

1 teaspoon\5 milliliters kosher salt

1 teaspoon\5 milliliters baking powder

½ cup\120 milliliters cold butter, cut into cubes

¾ cup\175 milliliters water

1 large egg

1 tablespoon\15 milliliters extra-virgin olive oil

1 yellow onion, chopped

2 cloves garlic, minced

1 pound\0.4 kilogram ground beef, chicken, or 2 cups\480 milliliters cheese

1 tablespoon\15 milliliters tomato paste

1 teaspoon\5 milliliters oregano

1 teaspoon\5 milliliters cumin

½ teaspoon\2.5 milliliters paprika kosher salt

freshly ground black pepper

½ cup\120 milliliters tomatoes, chopped

½ cup\120 milliliters pickled jalapeños, chopped

1 ¼ cups\300 milliliters cheddar cheese, shredded

1 ¼ cups\300 milliliters Monterey Jack cheese, shredded

egg wash, for brushing

fresh cilantro, chopped for garnish

sour cream, for serving

Pretzels

50 minutes | Makes 2 large pretzels

Ingredients

2 ½ tablespoons\37.5 milliliters molasses

1 ½ cups\360 milliliters warm water

2 ¼ teaspoons\11.2 milliliters active dry yeast

3 tablespoons\45 milliliters butter, softened, more for serving

4 cups\960 milliliters all-purpose flour, plus more for dusting

½ teaspoon\2 milliliters kosher salt

Pretzel salt for sprinkling, optional

Pretzel wash

2 tablespoons\30 milliliters baking soda

1 cup\240 milliliters water

TIP

For more servings, divide dough into 8 to 10 equal portions, invite some friends over and have a pretzel making party. Oven temperature and cooking time will be same as two large pretzels.

Discover recipes from all over the world!

Travel around the world from your kitchen.

Where do you want to travel next?